To Lisa

Enjoy the Journey

Julie Rosenthal

The Turquoise Lady

The Turquoise Lady

MY LOVES, FASHIONS, AND FORTUNES

Written by June Rosenthal
Illustrated by Kathy Hirshon

Terra Nova Books
SANTA FE, NEW MEXICO

Library of Congress Control Number: 2018945778

Distributed by SCB Distributors, (800) 729-6423

Published by Terra Nova Books, Santa Fe, New Mexico.
www.TerraNovaBooks.com

ISBN:978-1-948749-05-3

Thanks!

Thank you to:

Janet for her invaluable assistance with this book.

Jan and Reid for their sage input and loving support.

Ken for being there for Kathy 200%.

Jordan and Rhett, Riley and Jace for carrying forward our family traditions.

Dedicated

to

Kathy Hirshon

True—this will be a different kind of dedication because it will be more than just a name!

Kathy is a spiritual being—she has deep thoughts and an intuitive mind. Her ideas and how she expresses them are uniquely Kathy . . . lyrical cadence in prose.

Well, she cornered me over dinner one night and suddenly blurted out, "You need to write a book of short stories or vignettes of your exciting life, and I will illustrate each page."

I really gave some thought to her suggestion, but truly believed there wouldn't be enough interesting episodes to fill a book. However, I was intrigued, particularly with her offer to create art to accompany the stories.

Kathy is a world-class artist. She lived in Stamford, Connecticut, as I did, and was a really close friend. As a fine artist, Kathy needed to be in magical Santa Fe. She and her husband, Ken, happily relocated here, along with Rolf and I.

So it was Kathy who prompted me to write this book. It was all her idea! We have done this together, and it has been an exhilarating and enlightening process. . . and such fun!

We also had to learn about the publishing business, and it is a complex one. However, we now have our little book ready for the world. Kathy's artwork is exquisite—and her contribution to my vignettes is priceless. Together, we have something very precious to both of us . . . and hopefully to you, our readers.

Contents

Preface

I'm June . . . 94 and counting! It was such a joy to remember these tales and events, and to write the laughing, smiling episodes of my life for others to enjoy—and me too!

This is a story of me . . . a woman who rarely conformed to the norms for American women of my generation. Blazing my own individual trail helped me achieve goals big and small while relishing each adventure to the fullest. My attitudes were taught to me by my dear mother and father. It was their love that formed the loft of my soar.

LOVE . . . oh, yes, and so much caring.

LAUGHTER . . . always chuckles and grins.

Read with a light heart and gleeful joy. Live the episodes—as I did—in neither black nor white but definitely shades of turquoise.

And if you should find inspiration, so much the better!

A Healthy Philosophy of Life
Two Wolves

A Sioux elder is talking with his grandson—"Each of us has two wolves within us—one good, one bad. They fight constantly." The little boy asks, "Grandfather, which wolf wins?" And his Grandfather answers, "The one you feed, my son, the one you feed."

So it is in life—three giant steps to fulfillment.

Feed your good qualities—starve your bad.

Stay involved with life—from your early years to forever.

Don't be afraid to unplug the iPhone and tune out the television once in a awhile . . . it can be therapeutic!

The Guide

I t all started with a discovery when I was five or six years old growing up in Chappaqua, New York. I was an usher for notables checking out an Indian kitchen cave found by my brother in the dense woods behind my parents' property. These were my growing years with Native American history awakening in my young soul. I asked my mother to make a professional-looking sign for me so that people would know I was their true guide—and she embroidered "Guide" on the back of my sweater.

The Trapper's Helper

Instead of delivering newspapers like most young boys, my entrepreneurial brother, Harold, trapped muskrats and beaver to sell their skins to a St. Louis, Missouri, company. He set his traps at 4 a.m. before commuting an hour by bus to his private school. He employed me to pick them up because I attended the local school and got home at 2:30 p.m. each afternoon. So off I went into the woods two or three times a week to collect his animals wearing my father's huge hunting jacket with BIG pockets.

Even though I was only seven, I carried a pistol and knew how to use it! I would walk for more than a mile, carrying heavy, wet, dead animals in those big pockets. I was very proud to help my loving brother—and he paid me a nickel instead of a dime because it was bigger!

"Go West"

I was directly affected by the name of Horace Greeley, the nationally recognized newspaper editor who was from the Chappaqua area. (Our school was even named after him.) His famous nineteenth-century quote was, "Go West, young man!" Well, it may have taken eighty-eight years, but eventually I went West, young woman! However, in all those years leading to eighty-eight, I wore Western fashions in the East. Mr. Greeley would indeed be proud of this family—as our grandchildren, Jordan and Rhett, and our great-grandchildren, Jace and Riley, are living in Montana and growing up in "the West."

My Hero

My brother, Harold, was ten years older than I and had a lot of super friends. They took me everywhere like a mascot! One friend was six-foot-four, blond and "take-your-breath-away" handsome. When he was eighteen, and I was eight, he said that if I didn't date boys until I was sixteen, he would take me out on my sixteenth birthday. I promised—and sure enough, a few weeks before my sixteenth birthday (May 9, 1940), he called from London where he was serving as a captain in the RAF and told me that he had gotten special leave. Then he flew to the U.S. and drove to the country to take me out!

I was so excited! I picked out my most special dress and waited for the precious moment. He did show up, drove me to New York City for dinner and a Broadway show, "Hellzapoppin'." He looked like an Adonis in uniform, and I just never forgot that evening. What an incredible young man! Everett Wood—my hero!

World War II & Sox!

World War II interrupted my high school life like everyone else's—and I found myself entertaining our boys through USO gatherings and in other patriotic ways. A school group of us girls would be bused to White Plains, New York, about a half hour away, and we would spend the evening talking and dancing with our troops.

I never sat still long enough before to be a "knitter or sewer," but I learned to knit for our boys. The argyle socks turned out pretty good! We would occasionally bring a few boys back to our families for a home-cooked meal. Even at high school age, we all seemed to know the importance of winning the war.

Country Bumpkin & City Slicker

1942

—an interview at Katharine Gibbs, a business college in New York City. I arrived in blue and white saddle shoes and was quickly told that heels, stockings, skirts, and jackets were the uniform at this elite school . . . and this country girl had to conform. Again, my wonderful brother saved the day—he picked me up at Grand Central Station right after that embarrassing interview and whisked me down to Lord & Taylor's. Two pair of medium-heeled shoes in brown and blue, with handbags to match, then skirts, blouses and jackets were packed in a big bag. I felt like a celebrity!

The NYC Trading Post

While attending Katharine Gibbs, I used to walk from the school to Grand Central Station because I commuted from the country. There was a "trading post" store at Forty-Second Street and Lexington Avenue that fascinated me. I would window shop and sometimes walk in just to see the Western items, clothes, and jewelry. I finally spotted a gorgeous silver concho belt with turquoise, and I was hooked! The price in 1943 was $198! I asked the clerk if I could pay $10 a month, and he said "yes," so twenty months later, I wore it out of the store. It was my dream belt, and I never took it off! That was the beginning of my love affair with "turquoise" in any form.

The Dream Job

1944

and my years at Gibbs were over, so the following months were busy ones trying to find a job. The ultimate exciting position of secretary to the president opened up at the Powers Photo Engraving Company in Manhattan. It was a glamorous environment for a young woman. I really began to pay attention to my appearance.

My true dream was to work for a well-known fashion magazine. A year after joining Powers, a job opened up at *Town & Country* magazine as assistant to the fashion editor. Of course, I went for it and was hired! Again, those were fabulous celebrity-filled days of glamour and fantasy . . . utter joy!

After a few years at *Town & Country,* I was offered a position at *Vogue* magazine, which was the firm I had wanted to join right from the beginning of my original job search. I made the move immediately and stayed for many years, content and growing. Fashion now took on a new meaning!

A Friend Forever

I met one of my dearest woman friends of over seventy years right there at Conde Nast publishers. She worked at *House & Garden* magazine, while I was with *Vogue*. We met in the company elevator when she admired my cerulean blue jacket and skirt. Her name was also June, and we have kept in touch all these years!

The Horse Whisperer

Horses and I understand each other. Sometimes I feel like a "horse whisperer." Even strange horses nuzzle me, and the ones I ride follow me around when I dismount.

One vacation day in Palm Springs, I arranged a ride into the desert. The stableman asked if I would mind if a woman and man accompanied me on my ride. We three rode straight toward the mountains when suddenly the young man started to show off and was really abusing his horse. The horse reared and threw him off. I grabbed the horse's reins and made sure the rider was unhurt. I lectured him about the dangers of acting stupid on a live animal, and we rode back to the stable in silence.

Driving back to my hotel, I suddenly realized that my precious watch was not on my wrist. It was my twenty-first birthday special gift from my dad. I was devastated—and realized it must have come off when I grabbed those reins. Since it was almost dark, I had to wait until the next morning. I asked for the same horse I had ridden the previous day and rode toward the mountains again. The wrangler said I would never find it in the shifting sands. That handsome animal I rode led me straight to the place where we had all the trauma. The desert sands looked the same to me in every direction, but my horse seemed to know something I didn't. I looked down and saw something shining . . . Yes! My lost watch! I kissed my horse's soft nose, and we whispered to each other all the way back to the stable.

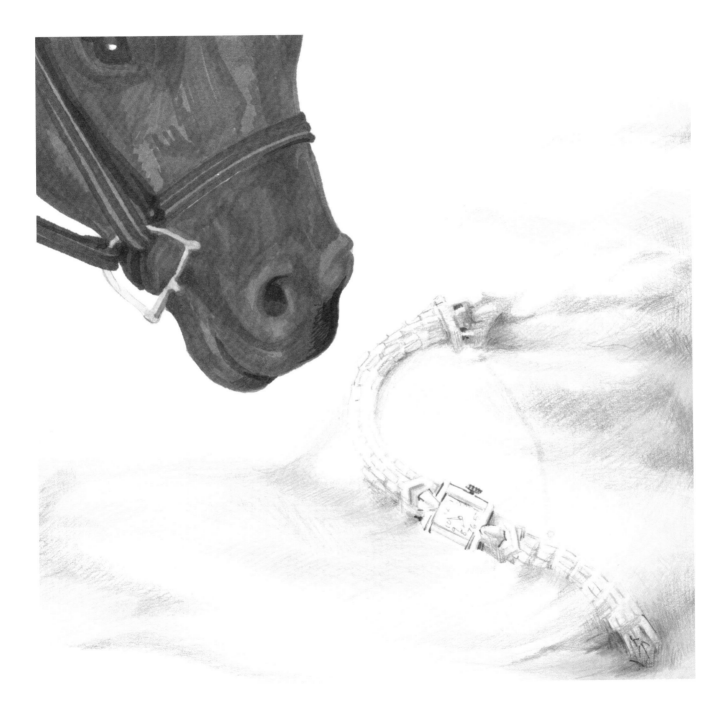

Forever Gold Lamé

1948

—I meet Rolf! That's where wardrobe really mattered because he worked in the fashion business, too. I was wearing a figure-revealing gold lamé evening dress when we met, and he carried a photo taken that night with him for fifty years, claiming for each of those years that this was a current picture of his wife! We met in 1948, married in 1950 and kept the knot tied for sixty-six years. He passed away late in 2016, but it wasn't six months prior to his death that he again mentioned that dress.

And the Bride Wore . . .

For my wedding in 1950, I really wanted a rose-trellis June wedding in my family's glorious rose gardens—but instead, I got April rains and an inside-the-home celebration! It poured all day and night—but evidently rain does bring good luck, because our union lasted sixty-six years! My wedding dress was indeed different, and particularly for 1950, when most women wore heavy satin, full-length wedding gowns with puffed long sleeves. That was the fashion then. My choice was waltz-length champagne lace with a Spanish mantilla head covering. It was designed solely by me. I wanted something unique, and attained my goal. Besides my engagement ring, I also wore my favorite turquoise ring. Rolf (don't forget he was in the fashion business) just loved everything!

Forbidden!

Our one-bedroom apartment in New York City overlooked Gracie Mansion, the mayor's home. I loved to walk and would make the trek from the East River and Ninetieth Street to Bloomingdale's at Fifty-ninth. I was given strict orders from Rolf never to walk farther south than Fifty-ninth Street in those pants, because "ladies" in New York didn't wear pants! And indeed, stores didn't even carry them! How perceptions have changed—today there are more "pant suits" sold than dresses!

"Very Pregnant"

Rolf was adamant about my not working after our wedding, so I left my fabulous job at *Vogue* to keep the peace. After a year, and only needing a few hours to clean a one-bedroom apartment, I was bored and wanted to go back to work. My dad and brother were in business together as fashion designers, so I talked them into hiring me to sell in their showrooms. In my second year working for them, I became pregnant. I felt great during my entire pregnancy and thought I looked fantastic. But in my ninth month, my dad said that I was truly looking "very pregnant," and he convinced me that it was time to stop showing designer clothes to buyers and stay at home to await the birth of my child. So I quit, and two weeks later, I delivered our son, Reid. I guess the expected norm for pregnant women in similar circumstances was confinement at home.

Born, Raised, and Married

Now Rolf insisted that I stay home and raise our son. We decided to spend a few summer months at my parents' home back in Chappaqua in the same colonial farmhouse where I was born, raised, and married. We stayed in the country during July and August when Reid was four months old. I really loved getting back to leisurely country living—and "Western clothes."

A Sad August

Unfortunately, August turned out to be a very sad time because my wonderful dad unexpectedly passed away at only sixty-two! He commuted to New York City in the morning and had a fatal heart attack in a restaurant that afternoon and never came home. A horrible shock—particularly to my mom—and we were very worried about her. Under the circumstances, we stayed on until October to keep an eye on her. Having her little grandson in the house seemed to help her spirits.

Of course, we all remembered the good times. I still see my dad at the grill every weekend. He loved to entertain and cook outside for his guests. He couldn't wait to don his apron and big white chef's hat! Memories can be so comforting . . .

Tragedy . . . Renewal

Fate has a way of determining one's life path. As Reid turned a year old, I decided it was time to buy a home in the country, and Rolf conceded. We found just the right house in Stamford, Connecticut, and moved in early June of the following year, 1954. The morning of our move, I received an urgent message from my mother that my brother's wife had died suddenly leaving three children, ages nine, five and the youngest at nine months. My mother then sold her home and moved in with my brother in New Jersey to help raise his three children. It is probably what saved her, as she was in a very depressed state of mind after my father's passing.

Lively Lola

My brother remarried after thirteen years, and his second wife became his business partner. They hired a lovely lady to help my mom with the teen-agers and household duties. Her name was Lola, and she reminded us of Hatti McDaniel: cheerful, positive, helpful. We all loved her instantly! Lola was known for her legendary fried chicken, and she also created the most charming folk dolls which she gave as gifts to many children and families. Lola's joyfulness enlivened the household!

A "Five-fer"

When Reid was six, we had a little girl, and we named her Jan. Both kids were great, and we were a happy family of four . . . five counting the dog. We loved our home, and I continued to enjoy dressing in "country clothes." These were mainly pants and westernwear, courtesy of my father's and brother's travels to the West. Cowboy boots, moccasins, and turquoise were my early trademarks.

A Western Fashion Plate

I used to drive to New Jersey with our two children and a large German Shepherd named Rex to visit the whole family there, and that's when we fell in love with Lola. She became a part of our extended family for many years. Later, my brother needed to live in New York City for business reasons, but that city move was not for Lola.

Rather than have this special woman leave our family for good, I decided to have her live with us in Connecticut for a few years while the kids were young. That "few years" turned into thirty-five! Even though she has been back home in the South for almost twenty years, she is still very much a member of our family. She was also a Western fashion plate on her own, loving the red and black cowboy boots we gave her!

Connecticut . . . Here We Come!

When we first moved to Connecticut, Reid was about fourteen months old. Stamford was truly a country town, and I felt very comfortable getting back to my rustic roots. My everyday clothes were ranch pants, Western-type shirt and perhaps a fringed jacket—sometimes Western boots or various beaded moccasins. It was such a natural look for me—but, of course, raised many eyebrows in this Eastern town! Others were wearing pastels, headbands, and the "preppy" look. However, I was entirely comfortable in my stunning Western clothes and thoroughly enjoyed the compliments that came my way.

A Love Affair with Turquoise

We lived in our first Stamford home for twenty-eight years and in the second one just a few miles away for thirty-four! We definitely weren't "movers." A young man was referred to me when we moved to our first house. He traveled West with his dad to Native American reservations and brought back jewelry to sell in the East. He would show up every four months with stunning pieces, and I must confess I bought something from him each visit. I still have most of his gorgeous turquoise and silver jewelry. To his credit they were truly authentic and very special. To give an example, I bought a silver necklace and attached pendant with a Sleeping Beauty turquoise stone from him for $55, and it was appraised recently at $1,750! My true collection of turquoise pieces actually started with this gentleman.

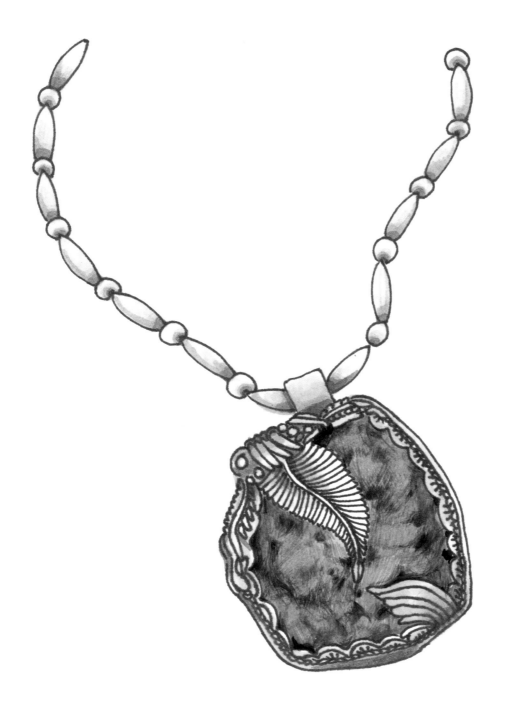

The Growing Years

The growing years of our two children went amazingly fast, as every parent knows. We had great fun which included a lot of family togetherness. We attended Reid's wrestling team meets and Jan's figure skating recitals. Of course, I was deeply involved with Reid's and Jan's school and athletic activities. I never missed any of their presentations and even braved catching a ride from a friend's son on the back of his motorcycle when my car wouldn't start. I was headed for a local summer camp parents' day for both kids. My late arrival was quite a sensation!

The Hunter and the Hunted

My father, brother, and husband were members of a hunting camp in New York State that belonged to a family of hunters. Of course, since my brother had taught me EVERYTHING, I became a hunter, too—almost the only female in those wild surroundings. They even built the "Hen House"—a small chicken coop-type structure, but I was glad to have my own quarters. Yes, I hunted with that crew for years until I awoke one day wondering why I loved carrying a rifle in cold dawn hours, tramping through the snow, and killing a buck—such a magnificent animal. I wrote a story which was published at that time called, "The Hunter and the Hunted." Writing helped me understand how I loved the chase and hated the kill. That was it. I gave up my gun and hunting for good.

A Cowboy Author

We also took our young son to our hunting camp in Roscoe, New York, and gave him his first experience in the true outdoors which inspired him to live in the West on his own working ranch, a life he still loves to this day. His love of the land (and this great country) inspired him as a brilliant author of "Threads West"—an award-winning, historic romance series. These books depict the European influx of people seeking land in the untamed American West during the nineteenth century. Anyone reading his books can feel his passion for life and the land.

Aha . . . Real Estate!

Okay—the first child off to college! I had made the decision that I wanted and needed to work again. My husband and I had a very serious back and forth over a Dairy Queen float—and I won! Now what job could I get that would allow me the hours to be at home for my daughter who was then twelve? A regular 9–5 office position was certainly not it. Something more flexible . . . Ah! How about becoming a real estate broker? Yes, that would give me the free time to be home at 3 p.m. when Jan arrived from school. And so, my career path was started at forty-six!

I received my broker's license just before Reid left for the wide-open spaces of Colorado. As a matter of fact, he became interested in real estate himself, especially after reading the 1970 real estate "bible," *The Principles & Practices of Real Estate*. He was fascinated, and guess what? Real estate did become part of his money-making endeavors in later years.

Branding Myself

So now it's the fall of 1970, and I have my broker's license. I wanted to be on my own as a broker instead of joining a real estate firm as an agent. However, at that time, I couldn't belong to the Multiple Listing Service system unless I belonged to an office. As I started out, I was enthusiastic and always had plenty of buyers, but listings were difficult to come by because they were all on the MLS for better exposure.

I did a lot of print advertising that first year and even found a boutique firm that let me show its MLS houses to my customers. I had a very good first year even with the huge competition of big name firms at the time, but I knew I had to be different if I wanted to stand out.

Of course, I wanted to be smart, truthful, compassionate, diligent in my work ethic, but I wanted to be recognized in the industry by branding myself in a completely different manner so that I would be quickly recognized and remembered. Easy! Unique Western fashion was the answer. No one else in the area styled themselves that way, and it was natural to me! My love of Native American jewelry and Western clothing made a very natural transition to my "business" attire, and very early attracted attention and remembrance.

Born . . . and One of a Kind

After the first year on my own, I did join that boutique firm, and about fifteen years passed very successfully with national recognition for me. By 1986, I decided that now was the time to open my own boutique real estate office. I found a perfect location—an 1840 one-room schoolhouse right on the most-trafficked main road in Stamford. I was nervous about owning my own office with all the large companies surrounding me, but again I was going to run my agency in a different manner than others, and it worked! It worked even better than I had hoped. I handpicked my great agents—and everything about our little office was unique . . . our building, our sign, the turquoise door, and our very special turquoise business card. In five words . . . "a one-of-a-kind" agency!

I was reminded by many that most wives of that era were homemakers and were not launching careers and businesses of their own. I truly felt it was my time to soar—and now, I also had my husband's blessing.

Incidentally, I am proud to say that special corner location now has a permanent sign that says, "Dedicated to Juner Properties."

On Getting Really Sick

November 1, 1985 was the day I decided to leave my fifteen-year employer to open my own real estate company, Juner Properties. I had a doctor's appointment that afternoon and discovered that I had cancer! I was determined to open my office in January of 1986 because it was slated to be a banner year for real estate sales—and indeed, it was. I physically struggled through that entire year until November, 1986, and then I knew I had to have the operation. Waiting all that time almost did me in, but Dr. Bernard Lytton of Yale New Haven Hospital saved my life. Optimism is such an indomitable factor in our lives. Dr. Lytton told me following the operation that I would not be back to work until the middle of the following March. I was at my desk on January 10, 1987!

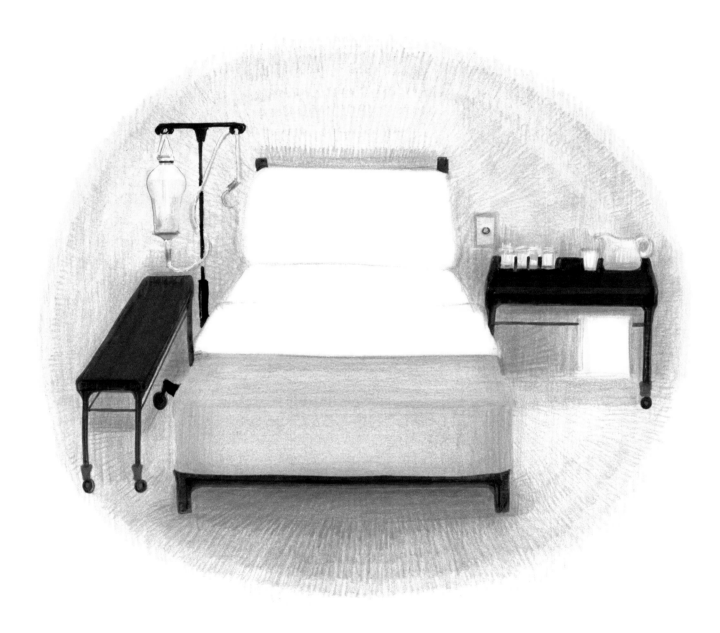

A Priceless 25-Year Run

Twenty-five years of a very special and successful family-type real estate office was the reward for our hard work and special "branding." Our fourteen brokers made an enormous impact on the marketplace and enjoyed a priceless run as Juner Properties! ("Juner" being June Rosenthal.) We were solid competitors with the national companies and gained a fabulous reputation as a specialty boutique. We made amazing sales and made many incredible friends. The branding stuck—anything turquoise was immediately recognized as Juner Properties!

Western Wedding in Connecticut

Our daughter, Jan, went to college in Colorado and stayed in the West after graduation. Rolf and I fully expected her wedding to be there since her fiancé was living there, and she now considered herself a Westerner. Surprise! Jan wanted a home wedding in Connecticut! So, we got busy . . . and came up with a Western theme carried out in the East. Jan wore a stunning white doeskin, fringed dress and canoed up the river to our riverfront steps. My ensemble was silk—a calf-length, purple, flowing skirt—matching purple and turquoise blouse and turquoise doeskin vest with hand-painted Native American symbols in silver and purple. Spirit of the Earth, right here in Santa Fe, created the vest from my design. With help from her father and father-in-law, Jan rose from the canoe and gracefully stepped up to the awaiting guests and ceremony. Meanwhile, our son-in-law, Jay, came down the hill on horseback. It may sound "hokey," but it was a perfect setting for those two. Soft Native American flute music in the background—the whole scene was mesmerizing and absolutely perfect for them! The pottery wedding vessel with two spouts (a gift from Rolf and me) was the final piece in forging exquisite memories.

Saleswoman Supreme

Our daughter, Jan, is an excellent saleswoman, as are most members of our family. (Remember my brother with the nickel versus the dime!) I really wanted her to join me in my real estate company, but she chose not to return to Connecticut after college, and instead entered the field of interior design. She and Jay have owned the beautiful Alpine Ambiance store and the Shady Deals window treatment company in Edwards, Colorado, for thirty years. The whole Vail Valley is their drawing card. She is a whiz at designing . . . and her favorite color . . . turquoise!

Giving Back

During my 25 years of building Juner Properties, I became very civic minded and held many great board and advisory positions with fine Stamford institutions. These included the Stamford Museum and Nature Center (cheers, Melissa!), ChildCare Learning Center, Stamford Land Conservation Trust, Stamford Historical Society and the Stamford Center for the Arts. Many other excellent organizations have benefitted Stamford, and I tried to say "yes" to all of them! Stamford Hospital is the very best. . . Ferguson Library is outstanding. . . Stamford Downtown Services is a brilliant concept (Sandy closes the main streets in the summer to allow incredible entertainment for all, with downtown Dine Around events the rest of the year!) There is also the charming Curtain Call Theater, the Bartlett Arboretum, the stunning Palace Theatre . . . and even our own fabulous Stamford Symphony Orchestra and the Connecticut Ballet!

I really wanted to give back just a little of what Stamford had given me. There were many fundraising affairs, and I attended everyone one of them, dragging my poor husband along. To top it all off, I was even named Citizen of the Year in 2007, which was a very special honor. Rick and Gary have elevated that celebratory achievement to its highest level. We enjoyed fabulous years of making new friends and enjoying many fun events.

...are grateful to...
...we continue to...
...we need all you can do...
...to support our services in...
...need
...in this
...community...
...we love)

Thank
you Mrs.
Gurba...

YOUR
MEANING...
GIFT HAS
MADE A...

Your continuing...
necessary
help...

Thanks to you
achieved our goal
again this ye...
critical
time.
Best

Annual Appeal!
Pl...

Dear Frien... Help...
Please consider incr—
your kind...

FUNDRAI...

...to follow up on the ide...
you shared at the board...
To help the organiz...
to benefit the comm...
we love the ide...
using the fund...
using. Your gi...

Once again, we are writing to
thank you for your time, energy
...support. Volunteering yo...
...nd generously donating
...serve the commun...
...we love!

Black, White, and Turquoise

Linda, a special business partner and beloved friend, wrote something truly meaningful in my "Citizen of the Year" journal. It went something like this: "All my life, I have been characterized as being too black and white—and not even a trifle grey—now I know someone who is turquoise, and it has helped me so much." I don't know what color black, white, grey, and turquoise would morph into, but if it improved that special lady even 1 percent, she would be 101 percent in my eyes any day.

Coat of the Century

When I first started in my own business in 1986, I was literally talked into buying a fur coat by one of my agents. Dorothy had her very famous fur designer at I. Magnin in Chicago call me to "find out about my lifestyle." I explained to her that it was oriented around turquoise, but I knew of no animal with turquoise fur (just being a smarty). Well, that furrier sent five coats to her New York showroom a few months later, and one of those coats was a turquoise mink! I kid you not! It was simply spectacular!

I couldn't believe that coat, and of course, I had to buy it! That could be the end of a great story, but there's more: My husband hated it and refused to take me out wearing that stunner of a coat. Quite a scene! But then one freezing New Year's Eve, we went to a huge downtown "Dine-around" event, and I insisted on wearing my nice warm mink. By the end of the evening, Rolf had decided it wasn't so bad after all because everyone who saw it raved about it! I've been wearing it ever since. Later, I had it transformed into a shorter, sheared mink car coat and still love, love, love it!

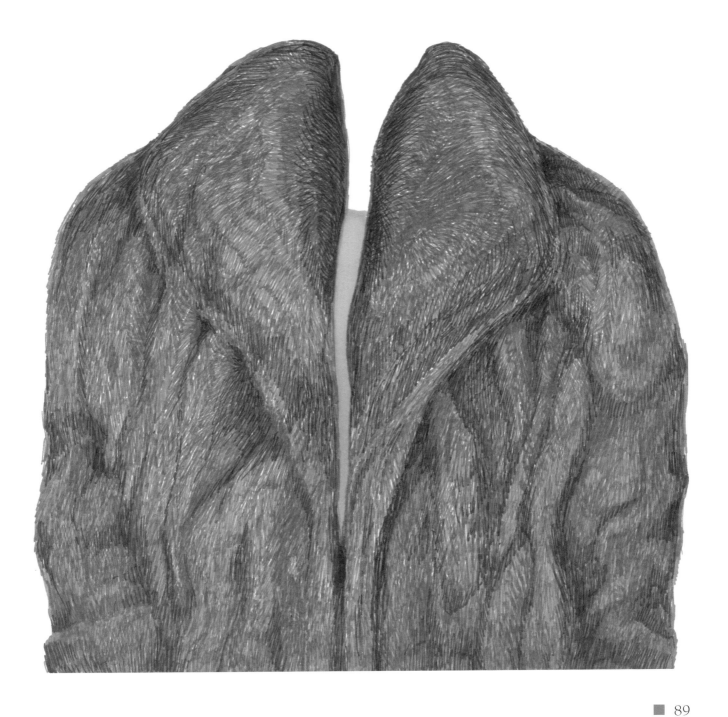

89

Cool Cars!

Needing a "statement" car to go with my "statement" wardrobe, in 1974, I purchased a white Jaguar sedan with white leather phone (the old fashioned big kind), and it was the talk of the town! I suddenly found myself with a lot of buyers, who (I think) just wanted to ride around in a Jag with a phone! I bought another new Jag in 1978 and again in 1981, both with white leather seats, a white leather car phone and a white leather video machine for the back seat that showed the properties we were about to visit. Those cars were so famous that the local *Stamford Advocate* newspaper ran a full, front-page picture of me in the last car with copy about the phone and video!

For further promotion, "Juner" was painted discreetly in turquoise on both front doors, and of course, my personalized license plate spelled out "JUNER." I still have a "JUNER" personalized license plate out here in Santa Fe, New Mexico, and what's even better is that the entire plate has a turquoise background as a commemorative of 1912 statehood!

A "Colorful" Experience

Very funny story—sometime in the early 1990s, I wanted to purchase a different car from the usual white Jaguar—an SUV which would be safe on our snowy and icy Connecticut winter roads. We shopped at Land Rover in another town after attending a Saturday tennis game in all whites. They only had black cars, and I wanted white, so they would have to order it for me. The salesman told us that their stock was very low, and they had received only one Land Rover in the previous weeks. He described it as a "God-awful" color which the dealership wouldn't even display in the showroom, so it had been retired to the mechanics' shop area in the back.

I asked what color could be so bad, and he said, "It's a green/blue, awful," and I said, "Can I see it?" So we walked back and took a look at it. Turquoise as turquoise could be! So, I bought it with a whopping $6,000 off the price! The salesman couldn't believe it! I had "Juner" painted in white as I described and a new phone installed. When I came to pick it up a week later, I arrived in full turquoise Western regalia, clothes, jewelry and all . . . and the salesman almost fainted!

Turquoise Forever

My turquoise "brand" really became known everywhere. One day a lovely lady from a nearby town who didn't know me called the office to tell me that she had seen a gorgeous turquoise pant suit in the Neiman Marcus window in White Plains, New York, about thirty-five minutes south of Stamford. She thought of me right away and went to the trouble of looking up my number and calling! An amazing and immediate connection through that distinctive color!

Camouflaging with Bling!

Turquoise just calls out to me! I walked into a shop in Barcelona, Spain, in 2010, saw these gorgeous turquoise pants—and, of course, bought them. I wore them proudly that night at dinner. The waiter tripped . . . and coffee in many places on my new pants! I brought them home, stains and all, and called on my friend, Tina, for help. She returned them a week later with all the stains cleverly covered with matching patches and a little bling! That lady could fix anything—and I am still wearing those pants with pride.

Turquoise Talk

Here's a brand new addition to my favorite color aura . . . a battery pack attachment for my iPhone so I always have double battery power. But what's incredible . . . our darling friend, Tim, found this useful, unique gift for me in—you guessed it!—turquoise! So now my phone is rimmed in my signature color—and even I can't believe it!

Doggie Shower

Doggies have always been family members in our household. In the beginning, they were beautiful German shepherds, and then after I started in real estate, we downsized significantly to Yorkshire Terriers or "Yorkies," as they are affectionately called. We had several beautiful little ones, and then in Colorado, we found a brother/sister pair (courtesy of their first loving mommy and daddy, Marji and Bill) who stole our hearts. We named them Rocki and Jazmin.

Judy and my office gave me an incredible "doggie shower," and what color do you imagine most of the gifts were? YES . . . "that" color! Their turquoise pillow is still used to this day. Little Jazmin always wore a turquoise bow, and Rocki sports a turquoise feather behind his ear. I was kept in good supply of these special pieces by the doggies' Darien groomer, Debbie, who made the bows and feathers for them to wear. She still makes and sends them to me periodically in Santa Fe. A special lady!

Gifts from the Heart

I have been sending a holiday card every year to about five hundred customers, clients and friends for the last forty-eight years. Included with each Western-themed card is a small gift that has the color turquoise in the gift or its packaging. I'm beginning to run out of ideas after all this time and may have to double back to early ones! I'm always on the lookout by February for the next holiday season!

Jumpsuit Dilemma

In San Francisco after a skiing trip to Heavenly Valley, Rolf and I took a stroll along the famous pier and wandered into the many shops. Not to waste a salesgirl's time, I told Rolf that I would ask if they had a turquoise leather jumpsuit (because no one would have that item!)—that way we could browse without being pounced on every minute. Well, it did work in five stores, but the sixth store's saleslady said, "I certainly do have a turquoise leather jumpsuit," and she brought it out from the back. Oh, my goodness—gorgeous, my size, and I was speechless and stuck! My husband was doubled over in laughter—and I bought it!

Safari Savvy

A travel adventure I would opt for every year if it were possible . . . an African safari. My first time was in 1980 in Kenya when we tented at Kitchwa Tembo on the Serengeti Plain. It was expertly planned by Abercrombie & Kent from beginning to end. Exhilarating, exciting, exquisite and never-to-be-forgotten . . . Cousin Ann (in the fashion business) sent me pants and matching jacket in two-shaded, soft and vibrant turquoise—and I wore that outfit on every morning and afternoon safari. Even many years later on a trip to South Africa in 2006, the animals came very close to our open Land Rover—and I would like to think this casual fashion statement pleased them as much as it pleased me. I wore it everywhere—not just Africa—for thirty-five years until it literally wore out!

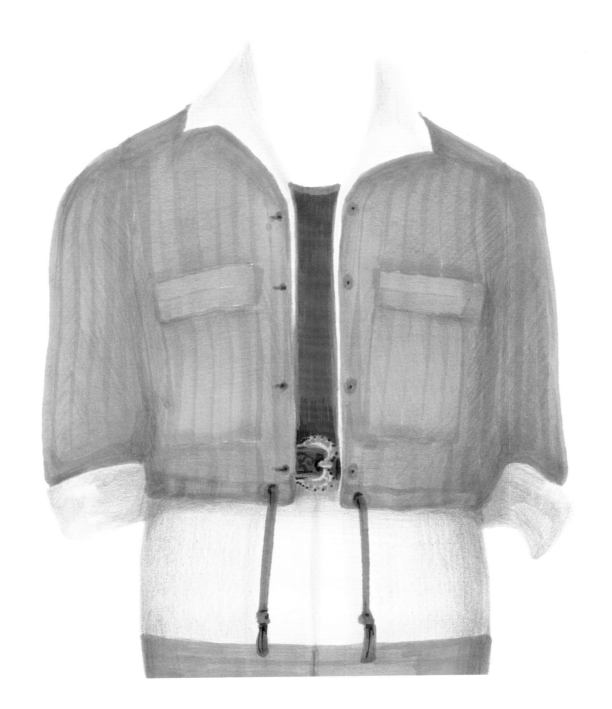

"Blue Man" Adventure

Then there was the "blue man" we met in Morocco. I was dead set on seeing this unique nomad, and then we saw one and spent an hour with him. Though we took a desperate chance to do so, we were young and full of adventure. All turned out fine, and here we are to tell the tale. The Tuaregs are called the "blue people" for the indigo dye-colored clothes they traditionally wear which stains their skin. It's not a turquoise color but a true cobalt blue. It was truly an experience of a lifetime. The whites of their eyes are blue, as are their fingernails . . . amazing!

Turquoise Trekking

Annapurna—with Everest in full view. Breathtaking, and we loved every minute of our four-day exploration trek from village to village on our way up the mountains in Nepal. Our very own special Sherpa, KC, and his band of helpers lugged tents, food and mini-comforts up the slopes! The days were all hiking, the nights for eating, relaxing, and storytelling. The mornings were magical with Mount Everest looming overhead straight up in the sky—mesmerizing and humbling at the same moment. These scenes have stayed with me and are sharper than a camera's eye. They will affect my soul forever. Unforgettable village scenes as yaks help with the rice harvesting. We would never want to lose touch with our incredible young Sherpa who watched over us—and we haven't!

Primitive and Provocative

In 2000, Rolf, daughter Jan and her husband, Jay, and I went to Papua, New Guinea. Wooden sticks through their noses—faces and bodies painted—huge hair wigs of their own hair . . . Those are the Huli Wigmen of Papua, New Guinea. It was hard to believe we were not on a movie set! Bev, our incredible guide, even arranged to get us into a funeral Maumau which are never attended by outsiders. Electrifying, stupefying, eye-boggling, spine-tingling and scary-beyond-belief scenes as hundreds of Wigmen carrying machetes and bows and arrows tended their fires on the plateau. The stench of the roasting pigs for the funeral feast and the odor of three hundred truly primitive people was overwhelming. That was how they settled murder from village to village. They have a "Forgiving Party," and no one gets punished! If I didn't witness this event, no one could ever convince me it took place. It is a fascinating but lawless country which we were privileged to visit once—and our photos will have to be our reminder, instead of a revisit.

Cow Stampede

Then there was a "cow stampede" in Stamford! Well, not really, but there was a huge cow display throughout downtown with an auction at the end of the summer, the proceeds going to charities. Each cow was artistically painted and decorated, and they were all so clever and beautiful. My cow was outstanding and a real tribute to—what else? Turquoise . . . Turquoise . . . Turquoise! Jewelry and all. My friends, true and famous artists, Jay and Gordon, did the work. They were my benefactors and did their usual spectacular job.

Giraffe in Poetry

Then a year later, we had a wild animal display—and I chose a giraffe. This time I asked my dear friend, Kathy, (the illustrator of these pages) to make my animal outstanding. Well, she did! He was called Longfellow and all the characters of "The Song of Hiawatha," that famous poet's epic poem, came alive when painted all over this giraffe. Exquisitely and uniquely finished, he brought the most money ever at our charity event. He was given back to me to place outside my schoolhouse office—and there he remains to this day.

Then my same artist/friend created "Dog Tales"—a large plaque of doggie tails (tales) in 100 percent turquoise. So clever and so appreciated by all, especially me.

Saddle Saga

In present day Stamford, we now have a downtown park—stunning, special, and world class, thanks to many, but in particular to our good friend, Arty, who tackled this huge undertaking and finally made it happen. Its new carousel is a beauty, and I grabbed one of the horses offered for charity and dedicated it to a friend who always wanted a carousel in our city but passed away before her dream could be realized. How to make it outstanding? The illustration on the opposite page shows how it turned out. Would you believe everyone knows who donated this gorgeous horse just by its saddle. Bless turquoise!

Cochiti Comforts

On my first visit in 1979, I fell completely in love with the spirituality of Santa Fe. Rolf and I revisited in 1980, 1981, and 1983, and I decided that we must own a little piece of this unique area. So in 1987, we bought a small home we called Cochiti, named after one of the Native American pueblos here in northern New Mexico. Our home was high on a hill in Tesuque with exquisite views of the Sangre de Cristo Mountains and the foothills. It's priceless and so special—small, high-ceilinged with two bedrooms and lots of windows facing south.

We spent ten to fourteen days there every September, and the kids came from their Western homes to help us enjoy this treasured place. Because of its privacy and stunning charm, we had many celebrities renting during the year—James Michener finished his book *Hawaii* on our terrace . . . Robert Redford spent many weeks there . . . Elizabeth Taylor was a guest, and even Hillary Clinton enjoyed a few nights' stay. We still own it and have spent many beautiful weekends there after relocating permanently to Santa Fe in 2013.

Santa Fe Spirituality

Santa Fe just reached out and drew us in to her unique and utter charm. One-third Native American, one-third Hispanic and one-third Anglo—very diverse cultures, and they work at getting along. Might just be a lesson for the rest of the world. High desert at seventy-two hundred feet of elevation is its geographic description, and the soft curves of the historic adobe architecture create a warm aura over "The City Different." The brilliance and clarity of the light has drawn artists since the nineteenth century and gives the region a magical spirituality. Its dynamic magnetism pulls one into its inner soul. It has a life all its own, and it permeates . . . head to toe, inside and out.

The Kingdom of El Castillo

At eighty-eight and ninety-one years of age, it was time to decide how to live and where to live out the rest of our lives—many choices including staying right where we were in Connecticut. Rolf would have nothing to do with retirement home communities—"I am not living the rest of my life with old people!" And this at ninety-one! I found El Castillo ("The Castle" in Spanish) in downtown Santa Fe, a five-minute walk from the Plaza, through my friend, Mindy, at Desert Son. Actually, I found this adobe-clad, pueblo-styled, gardened courtyard architectural beauty to be everything I could ever want in a home. And my hopes of its residents and staff equaling the beauty of this Santa Fe life-care community were answered. Everything one could ask for, and only a few minutes' walk from the center of town and all its sights! Certainly one of our best decisions ever!

About the Author

Born, raised and married in her family home in Chappaqua, New York, June Rosenthal's ties to the earth, nature and all things natural came at a very early age through the wise guidance of a mother and father who allowed her unique childhood experiences— along with an adored 10-year senior brother who taught her everything "outdoorsy." Her family, their bonds with the land and her own inquisitive, indomitable spirit molded a confident soul which fueled an adventuresome young woman.

At 20, her trapper and guide's garb of adolescence evolved 180° through her job at *Vogue* magazine which opened the door to fashion and travel . . . the loves which have been touchstones of her high-energy life. However, her marriage to Rolf in 1950 and becoming a mother to son, Reid, and daughter, Jan, were her ultimate joy.

At 45, residential real estate beckoned, and helping others became yet an additional fascination. Her turquoise aura was noticed by all, as she adorned her outfits with it, whether casual or formal. It was in the swirl and bustle of her accomplished real estate career (now 48 years and still working), that the true beginning of her brand emerged . . . "The Turquoise Lady." That powerful blue/green stone became a Connecticut household password amongst her many loyal customers, clients and friends, who remain the highlights of her life to this day.

This little turquoise memoir book is meant to portray June's remarkable lifelong journey of 94 years. Hopefully, it will inspire the aging who may believe that achievements fade as one grows older—and also inspire the youth to believe that anyone can achieve and make their mark if they invest the time, energy, work and imagination that dreams demand and success requires.

Take it from The Turquoise Lady—the elder years can be the best years—a positive outlook is what matters most.

About the Illustrator

Kathy Hirshon graduated from Fontbonne College in St. Louis, Missouri, and moved to New York City. She enjoyed a career in magazine publishing, working for the Hearst Corporation and Time Inc., among others.
Marrying Ken Hirshon in 1992, she moved to Stamford, Connecticut. There the Hirshons met the Rosenthals and fast became friends.

Kathy painted murals, taught art at Bi-Cultural Day School and created a solo exhibition for the Bartlett Arboretum. Her show, "Spirited Trees," inspired the book *Echoes: Listening to the Voices in Spirited Trees* by Michelina Docimo.

The Hirshons now live in Santa Fe, where Kathy's fine art, her charred narratives which are painted and burned into wood, have been represented by the Gaugy Gallery on Canyon Road. She illustrated *The Turquoise Lady* as a gift for June Rosenthal, the real Turquoise Lady, with love!